more than

THREE
FEET
OF
ICE

more than

THREE
FEET
OF
ICE

BRENDA SCHMIDT

thistledown press

Library and Archives Canada Cataloguing in Publication

Schmidt, Brenda, 1965–
More than three feet of ice / Brenda Schmidt.

Poems.
ISBN 1-894345-89-4

1. Canada, Northern—Poetry. I. Title.

PS8587.C45588M67 2005   C811'.6   C2005-900873-3

Cover and book design by Jackie Forrie
Printed and bound in Canada on acid-free paper

Thistledown Press Ltd.
633 Main Street
Saskatoon, Saskatchewan, S7H 0J8
www.thistledown.sk.ca

Thistledown Press gratefully acknowledges the financial assistance of the Canada Council for
the Arts, the Saskatchewan Arts Board, and the Government of Canada through the Book
Publishing Industry Development Program for its publishing program.

For Harvey

CONTENTS

1'

2'

3′

The North is the Canada that was, the Canada that could have been, and the Canada that is not.

— Kerry Abel and Ken S. Coates
"Introduction: The North and the Nation",
Northern Visions: New Perspectives on the North in Canadian History.

1'

Go Beyond

Is it the artist's shadow
or the artist's dream

hovering there above the willows
drifting over the water

— John V. Hicks, "Fantaisie"

An answer hovered here
as I slept in the cliff-shade. It came
in the whine of diamond drill: *ever*
beyond the rock is water. The feverish
air of yesterday lies still in a wet bed of sedge,
        fills every hollow stem.
Willows bend, cup the pond, and water lilies
float in milk so pure it loses its need to be
white or milk or swallowed.
If somewhere earth hides a mouth it might
welcome cool smooth petals on its tongue, blow
blooms held above water off their thrones, peel
the gold off stamens, eat anything perennial
found coated in light, even the song sparrow
who calls my name in a language I imagine
evolved from something wingless, a few
ounces of life in flight that will land
just long enough to nest in a thicket, hatch
a promise that will fledge when I'm asleep
or maybe when I'm making love. Ever
will things float between rock and water,
branch and bird, touching nothing but air.

A Wasted Spring

Black spruce stand gaunt, bark naked.
No one wants to know how full things could have been.
Light hangs on boughs, fills gaps between needles,
deepens the bark's curl with rough shadow. Resting
on the trunk in early morning, a hand is unlabelled,
its anatomy pinned to wood with sun; held
in the air it makes a rabbit's shadow hop from
tree to tree. It's skinny, as if it, too, is
starving.

A dry fall, a long winter, a cold spring
unfold like warnings. These days I pack lightly,
backpack, dog-eared bird guide, black binoculars
dotted with peanut grease, the remains of water
that washed yesterday's dinner down.
It's only a mile walk from the truck to the lake,
and a ten minute boat ride to the cabin
to check on things again.

Last week the forest purged thin bear, pried loose
the black coats still glued to the ground under tree-fall.
From a collage of root-bound dirt and grass, a hunger
pulled free and moved from low sun to low shadow, uprooting
rotting logs, consuming whatever might have squirmed underneath.

Everywhere I saw signs I've seen before: blond scars on spruce,
black scat, overturned rocks, but for the first time the tracks led me
up the path from the dock to the cabin, to the plywood
ripped off the window, to a mess of broken glass, to paw prints
stamped in blood among Fruit Loops on the kitchen floor.

ALONE ON A BOREAL STAGE

Four days off and all I do is come out here.
Not far from work, not far from town, but far
from what I want.

Here loneliness knows its audience, expresses itself
in a twist of root running bare over stone,
where the rock wrist bends
                                    over the horizon
and slash marks still ooze under
a rain-soaked scab of leaves.

Here, in the crack between my legs, dirt
huddles in corners away from all light. I fear
the space will grow
ferns or moss or something I cannot name.
I look into the sun, close my eyes and see
spores floating like balloons out of reach.

The stick I whack doesn't mouth back, cannot
help uttering sounds of the beaten.
Here faint echoes across the swamp fade
before the sun, and a phoebe watches silence
struck from a dead spruce in-between.

Cliff Lake

A yellow rail calls from the marsh below the trestle, answers
the click of pebbles in my palm.
Its rhythm is clear, measured, as if a song
should be that hard, as if, in the dark, or
because of it, this bird knows best
how rock should sound.

Over there is the rock on which I used to stand
long before I'd dive into the lake. I can't see the cliffs now,
but the water below is dark as any memory of surfacing.
                    Tonight I walk here because
the land on either side of the tracks is known to save
the paths of animals in dirt. I know the locomotives
that force hooves and claws to rub roots
sprawled across the trails. All night roots shine
around the boot scuffs.

Walking here is an act of preservation. Creosote
treats the mind, tie by tie, slows rot, gives me something more
to walk on. The odour binds another time to anything moving
along the moon-lined steel. In the dark
I see the beauty of what's constructed; only in the dark
does it smell like it should.

A Game Southerners Play in the North

Simon Says, a colonial game everyone's tired of playing,
yet on the periphery I still hear a voice and see people
acting on command, as if saluting, not wanting
to be singled out as ones who can't follow.

Simon says stand still!

We act like trees dead on the edge, or ones barely alive and leaning
at various angles to the ground, posed like strategies
pushed by wind into failure's slow fall, as if we could actually feel
the frontline chainsaws revving, the wood chip spray, the sawdust
sticking to bark on adjacent trees, and simply fainted instead.

Simon says face south!

We're hungry. All the activity leads to unquenchable thirst.
Between hot rod wrappers and beer bottles, we mimic wildflowers,
stagger in shadows, stumble outside the lines, throw seeds
at one another, at birds, at these bare legs. Here it's no crime
to stick stamens out at order and scatter in the darkness,
roll in a hole underground, thrive in dirt. We give not a damn
about how things grow, about soil, its poverty, the games played in it.

DISLOCATED

In a circle of willow a mourning warbler sings
an unfamiliar hymn.
                              I hear it
when I stop the car to pour more coffee,
stretch my legs, and I follow the song
through the ditch, over
the smell, the sponge, the wet of it.
The hooded head is dark in shadow, body so yellow
it pulls away at the neck. Half lost in leaves
I almost believe it's my ghost, the dislocation
a reflection of the things inside that were
forced into unnatural positions. Light
this apparition's song, as if it knows
hope is being chased through the bush like a bird
never before observed. Beyond the center of the trees'
summer droop, beyond backlit feathers,
the clutch of perch, the bounce of branch
suddenly deserted, it throws its voice.

THE ANIMAL OF MORNING

Some say there's danger in spending too much time alone,
but they don't know how a clearing offers space
empty of the usual — see, its periphery can be
a treed edge of vision, the breath of things moving
through branches as silently as raptor wings. Right now

I need to see the great grey owl fly overhead, a morning, a life
compressed in the air-brush of its wings — fear of grief, the end of it
might flap across the sky with hope buried like a feather's quill in flesh.
Anything beyond is lost in a vole's slow blink, in its struggle,
the soft belly, cinched-in bill like a New Year's cracker,
to be pulled apart to cheers for the prize inside.

I need to see the vole's legs, limp as the coming days, but pinker,
hang in the air like a god's above the sedge it ran through; see
each eye carry a dot of dawn, a smudge of the first light before
the owl descends and folds itself into the forest, into
the whuf of young waiting in spruce at sunrise,
the stick-rattle of hunger nested on the edge that arises
from the pantomimed rip of flesh before the prey is delivered.

ANOTHER LOGGED STAND OF TIME

As years fall, time — what has passed, what's left — is divided
into eight-foot lengths, loaded on a truck, hauled south.

In a clear cut, black spruce can trip anyone, its exposed root
curved, dirty and hard. Stumps
crawl with bugs that overwhelm
any desire to name them.

It's night, but I can still see the new clearing
a mile or so from the cabin, just outside the beard of trees
they left around this rock-lipped lake.
Log will strike log
till sleep finally comes. As I wait it occurs to me
that erect trees differ little from the fallen.
Wood is wood, bark and sap incidental,
the chainsaw buzz, the skitter roar just sound,
but it's the daylight through the narrow strip of trees
left between the road and what was logged
that few ever see, the sunlit roots curled
like claws of something still digging, a reoccurring
dream buried alive, dying somewhere
between grave and surface,
unable to dig itself out.

In the Face of What's To Come

Houses stick up like bits of skin on the land's chapped lips,
the smokestack a rotten tooth in a Halloween smile.
Everywhere there are signs of faulty occlusion.
In rock-deflected wind a faraway voice
warns us not to come here.

But we keep coming back. The money is too good.
On days off we head to the lake, build a dock, dig
a new outhouse hole, hoping the wilderness
will take the place of what we've left behind.

The first year the forest pulled us through itself
so fast we didn't know we'd moved. Still the dirt clings.
It wasn't until the discovery, beside the trail between
the lake and rock, of a single fiddlehead, a fern set to spring,
that something new unfurled. Who knew expectation
could be wound so tightly around nothing and still grow?

Ferns no longer lace the hollow's shadows. Every spring
we build and dig while the same birds perch in trees that lean more
and more toward the ground's lowest point. It's there we scrape
the earth as if it were a plate only to find we've struck bottom.

After Years of Slowing Down for Frost Heaves

Salt shakes the highway ice loose, ending the potential
to slide into these steep ditches. The car is white; I get it
on my jeans. Home is yet another hour down a road narrow
as a snow-packed marriage. It's nothing but frost heaves.

Rules of the road: before a bump sign pull over, consider
another leap into darkness, how slow to go to avoid bottoming out.
Breathe in black spruce, exhale willow, choke on fumes.

Traffic speeds by within inches of my legs, tire spray fine
as anything that passes. Like a hand in the night or time
over discord, it films everything behind, everything ahead.
Foot in a puddle, mind in mud, I stir up a cataract to cloud
the sky's reflection, your face, blur things even more.

Eyes, still in motion, skip across the road and back the same
way we've bounced over time, crossing paths and enlarged hearts
with flat stones, a side-arm throw. Twenty years later, still driving
back, still kids searching for the right rock at the edge of a slough

or by a road-salt puddle where pupils constrict like hope and irises
ripple with colours so close to asphalt, to us. Our skid marks
covered with mineral grit, its crystal structure, the same old acid-base
reaction wedged between a frost heave's peak and tires launching.

Among Convicts Clearing Scrub

It's not the quick glance, eyes hitting the windshield
like stones, or the spider cracks running from the chip
in the soul, the light caught, the startled vision, or the ditch
he stands in, the wall of tree behind, the prison's barbwire roll
mosquitoes, the twisting black fly cloud above his head.

It's not how light rides the back of man, axe in hand,
hacks a path through trees, cleaves the darkness
like a chicken, blade deep in fat-pebbled silence.

It's not the highway, a keloid scar, an asphalt-sutured laceration
healed, yet enlarging, edged with willow clipped like hair
that's not allowed to grow back. Some prefer old wounds
to be uncovered — in the forest they shine white as any bum.

It's not the ditch's reek — like beer bottle sludge pouring
out of a passerby's straight-ahead yellow-line stare — or the way
smashed brown glass catches light as if hope's sharp pieces
were scattered between the busload of men hacking willow.
Fear's a ditch where bugs suck blood, where labels stick
to broken bottles, where everything cut will grow back wild.

But it's the moment before stone hits, the moment you see it.

CROSSING ATHAPAPUSKOW

How still the lake, breathless, a deep breathing-space
the enormity of August stretched so tight it could not move,
so tight the bones of men, their ghosts, almost poke through.

Led by a guide, he returns at dusk, canoe-bent, washes the bush off,
removes dark things from between his toes and crawls into bed
without eating, stomach already full. Under covers his belly growls
in the dugout beneath his ribs. All night wolves howl back.
Some things cannot be digested, some bodies of water
cannot be crossed alone. It's true—-water marks
thousands of crossings with nothing but diminishing waves.
Hope, a paddle cutting water in silence, pushes the vessel along.

All night he lies eyes open, while moonlight floats across pupils,
crosses veined regions, places Hearne knew well. At times
he, too, would lie crumpled like a piece torn from a parchment map,
knowing the vital portages were inked on a soul not his.

NIGHT ON AN OLD TRADE ROUTE

The fire dies,
Here we feed
In the dark one
more alike, light
skin in
eyes adjust
your dark
across the room,
space like soot

the cabin is black.
the silence.
would think we'd be
failing to separate
a spectrum. In time
I begin to see
form emerging
the grey
in-between.

ACUTE ANGLES DRAWN FROM A STORM OVERHEAD

No space for a gasp between lightning and thunder under this
downed tree — its trunk offers little shelter in the right
triangle formed with stump and ground. Even with points known
it's hard to measure angles in a downpour or search for anything
possibly isosceles when rain beats leaves down.

A trapper once said she spent a summer in this forest, slept on hides,
studied geometry, met Euclid, learned storms in ancient Greece
still create static in the mind and out of every orifice
intra-cloud lightning can emerge as common notions.
Anyone who sees lightning strike a tree knows
the whole is greater than any splinter,

those struck forever measure space charged. She said
after lightning struck her snare she has fried rabbit but fails
to duplicate the tenderness, the taste — perhaps the electric
hare forgot its foot was caught when it saw the light — oh to be
that relaxed when hair stands on end.
If trapped in a storm it's best to curl around the angles,
the assumed properties of space, and wait
                                    for the clouds to move on.
Never count the seconds between flash and bang
and divide.

TRAPLINE

There must be a safe way out
among the stumps, between branches.
Indentations of feet that passed through here
a thousand years ago
fit mine like shoes, the kind that could pull
a lifeless soul down to the bottom of a lake.

Think the path and it will appear
as one of many well-trod routes; these grooves
in the nails of the past point to some deficiency
still undiagnosed. They invite examination, a cautious step.
Horizontal ridges can mean many things, or nothing —
it depends on the way you look at them. It's like
the doctor I once knew who would hold a patient's hand
so close to his face you could see
the fingers in his eyes. In reflection
everything was smooth.

It's when a person is lost you notice
how many directions there are to go, how
the feet tend to sink while orientation becomes
a position less and less true. When you begin
to go in circles, arriving at the same place
again and again, something other than ghosts
moves into daylight like it's home, turning trails of hope
into traplines with steel jaws spread wide, concealed
inside. Things that press get caught.
When leg-hold traps snap shut
they never let go.

Breaking Trail

A bull moose slips from a gallop across the highway, sun slides
          over its back, hits asphalt as the animal
finds balance and runs, belly whacking cattails in the ditch.
The suck of leg in mud echoes off rock,
fuzz floats long after the moose disappears, a bit of hair
sticks to a splintered trunk. How long has it been?
The last moose I saw around here
was in the back of a truck, its head jiggling
on top of a body gutted, quartered and stacked.

          The path is obvious.
A willow stick works to doctor tracks, remove the ridge
pushed up by cloven hooves. Remodeled
          holes give no indication of direction.
Wet dirt is a slut. It's too easy
to follow what has already moved through.
A stick exposes roots of wildflowers, weeds, the family of grass,
the subtleties of separation, what it means to grow.
Track by track I dig toward the forest edge, disappear
          in trees

and re-emerge. Sun lies on my head and a found grey
antler. A fingernail runs along each crack as if seasons
          past could last in space. Sun falls off,
lands in a puddle at the bottom of a dug-out hoof print.
There I watch it drown.

The Hunt

Mud smuggled in hoof-splits lies between holes,
obscuring the tracks of hunters who came before me.
Weaving through the bush, I am a thread needled
by the blood-drunk hum of mosquitoes.
Willow slaps my face when I look down.

It's not the first or last I'll follow:
this young bull with the lame hind leg,
heading north just like the dream,
bits of antler velvet left behind like crumbs.
Wolves lick them; between the fingers
they feel like tongue.

In the fall I'll hide beside the trail in a blind of willow;
I'll blow rolled birch bark into sound and wait
for the crash of animal through bush, for the finger
jitter to settle into trigger, for the exact muscle ripple
to find my eye in the crosshairs, to find the pupil
dilating with prayer for the kill.

Cabin Fever Symptomatology:
Yet Another William Blake Dream

Daylight sullies the reason why you pointed a shotgun at my head, pulled the trigger, yet missed at such close range; why the shell fell out of the barrel intact; why I took a moment to imagine the type of shot packed beneath its crimped end; why, instead of running or pleading, I shot back, my gun launching blue Bic pens that pierced your chest, spitting out blood as they bit into your heart. Yet you did not die, but grew instead into this screaming wide-eyed morning.

A Door Left Open

The door between the north and south blew open
the day Mr. Rock flew in to bless the marijuana operation.
From this rock you could see a space as the jet came in.
It's the closest I'll ever get to a federal minister,
                    that kind of power,

a dream on greenstone in the middle of nowhere,
in a place the glacier scraped clean; it's a fly-speckled place
full of swatters and things get squashed, reduced
to resources, nonrenewable as words, the ore that is
mined out of silence.

He flew out again the same day, after injecting
the region with a dose of attention, a vaccination
                    against communicable disease,
against this need to absorb the pores, the openings
in skin, in leaf, in rock, to be the interstitial space
between what's unseen. See how the south swells like an arm
when intravenous fluid seeps from vein into tissue.

The door cracked open again
when he appeared on the late night news; a quick clip
showed the minister in the mined-out shaft
hundreds of feet down, looking around, his face
hidden in the shade of a hard-hat; yet in a mine of dreams
he is more: something that waits behind rock, hides
behind spruce needle, tree branch, shifting song of the hermit thrush,
dusk-bound sky, behind the ant that carries my skin away in bits
to reconstruct me underground where I grow so thin, so long
the tunnel cannot contain me and I burst
                    out of the holes like broken thread.
Still I know he's there, on the south side, just out of sight.

A Midnight Tour of Dark Places

Many years stamped on the back of coins are unexplored.
I pick pennies off the ground at night and fill my pocket.
This is the north, a place where loose change is easily found,
where dirty fingers smell of copper.

On this street coins drop. In rooms above, nuns once rocked nights
full of feverish babies and pneumonia staked more claims than men.
The hospital, long abandoned, its cement walls jaundiced, rises
into its halo like a well-loved saint while its foundation falls
into the depths of its cracks and shadows.

North of here I could find more pennies where men used to spend
the same nights paying the same women. Under the streetlight
they're easy to see. But no one cares to walk there anymore.
On the long dark stretch between the dimmest and brightest light
I miss a fortune. There I walk so slowly even the old stars
shoulder me aside on their way by, yet still not find a thing.

THIS BED OF STONE

Our bodies lie under a cadaver sky
sutured with smelter smoke.
Get used to the smell.

In the rocks above the path we're like gods
watching tourists read elaborate signs
that explain basalt rock formation.

Our lips dry together and sulfur stung tongues
stuck in each others mouth define dioxide.
Skin on skin we recreate the hump of rock

we lie on. Volcanic pocks and cracks imprint
our bare flesh, a shallow indication of something
atmospheric, maybe molten.

POINTS OF INTEREST

1. The Crosses

Two crosses cemented to a rock-cut in the ditch,
a hand on greenstone left behind
in paint. Fingers lost in cracks and pores
point to a wreath of poppies, how red
plastic fades in the sun.

A still wet coat of white
now covers the layers peeling
free of the wood; it thickens the curls
where brush hair sticks.

> *Tips for tourists: You won't find*
> *a ditch free of such markers. You*
> *won't find one person free of its marks.*

2. The Cemetery

Someone decided Jesus should hang
in the cemetery, back to a wall of rock.

From there no one can see
the names on the headstones.

A raven perches on the right wrist, watches the lighter
shadow of a bird move across the stone chest

while he tears bits of meat from a bone;
a piece falls on the hand and slides down a finger

to the ground, leaving a pink streak that drips once
as it follows the direction of descent.

Tips for tourists: Look closely
at the backside of this sculpture, see
how the marble buttocks sag
when you stare through expectations.

3. The Rock

Greenstone lying under snow is
the ancient body winter shrouds.
White powder piled on the face
covers the rough edges in the rock
          hardened by a fire
unlike the kind lit now. The flame
hides inside a sliver of cold stone,
no longer moving through
          narrow veins.
Blood flows slowly this time of year,
under three feet of snow
a bit of ice and quartz touch.

*Tips for tourists: Dig a hole, touch
the uncovered rock, see if it feels
the same as the stone you use to weigh
down your heart.*

4. The Path

In spring the rock around town is a tongue
of a dry dying man refusing water.
A shallow breath passes over.

It is March, a month
not an order, a bearer of spring
no longer burdened with snow.

A stick dragged across the path
leaves a light dividing
line of wood dust. On greenstone

a trail of cream brings a raven down
to rise again in a moment
weighted with thirst. Bits of dead

wood ground down on rock
cling to its feet, then fall.

Tips for tourists: Avoid making contact
with the feet of dead birds. The claws might
grow in absence, might puncture your skin.

5. The Other Path

Mining fills the shafts with intention, every day
with metal-bearing rock. The surface shivers
over timed blasts, more ore drops
underground. Naked and alone
a path by the graveyard crosses
over the place where men shove
sticks of dynamite and wait.
    Bodies absorb the moment, a detonation
moving earth inside time, in another space
full of sharp edges where rock bolts hold
walls in place while miners scoop up the rubble.
Shift after shift, the endless tremble
when the empty truck goes down, the loaded rumble
as it circles back to the surface.

*Tips for tourists: To fully experience vibrations
passing through your body, close your eyes
until you see lashes, and hold.*

6. The Graves

Mounds of dirt on the graves match
this land, the curve of rock. Outstretched
arms do not link the two.

In the dirt, drawings of the horizon
include a few black spruce that rise from cracks
into clouds dug deep in the soil.

Between dirt trees a stick figure
points to where a half-buried stone stands
beside footprints that sink so deep
the feet must have been pulled.

*Tips for tourists: Wait until the dirt sinks,
until the rain washes the family's footprints
into the tractor tire tracks, before stepping
on the earth tears seek.*

7. The Wreckage

A strip of chrome on greenstone:
        its gleam can be caught
on the highway, on the curve
from where it flew.
The sound of traffic travels
across the swamp and up the rock
to touch the twisted metal.
Beneath the wreckage a shadow
sun shapes into something
so dark, so close to human
it makes heads turn
        the other way.

Tips for tourists: Please leave
artifacts in situ. Whatever items
you take home will bear
loss; like a premature baby,
it will lie wrinkled in your palm,
helpless and dependent
on you for life.

WHAT I FIND AT MUSEUMS

Red petunias bake in the garden by the museum door.
The plot's pale face cracks
          the sun between plants.
While I wait, petals, edged black,
become ash in my fingers.
I want to go inside to see the artifacts
the community has collected; I want to see
what people leave behind. A sign
says *Welcome Visitors* and *Open*, yet
the door is locked, as it was
last Saturday and the Saturday before.
Windows remain barred, the door
a grey display of contemporary hardware.
Perhaps *Hours of Operation* refers to somebody's
appendectomy or bypass, an opening
other than the one expected here.

Further down the road another museum
is simply padlocked shut, no sign
to indicate anything.
By the door I find more red petunias, and more
withering.

A Northern Equation

So many faces linger in the wood smoke on Big Island, so many
conversations shortened, unresolved. No matter how I multiply
lake times rock times trees times years and divide
the product by the number of dead,
the quotient never reflects the number of times
I am contained. Infinity rises
from burning logs, blows across the lake.
Nothing is insular here.

Here a pupil does math with the body
spread over October stone, feels the cold
climb the spine, breaking the only rung unmoved.
Algebra offers no general statement of relations:

a (broken rung) = b (broken ladder) = c (no sure way
          to ascend) = d (descent,
a whole other matter. A simple slip
on wet rock, the waiting lake below, between
some geometry unmeasured. A fall,
rarely rectilinear, is more of a range within
which even bears fail to move in straight lines as they drag
grubs from under logs with a curved sweep of dirty
claw and move on, feet licked clean of the squirming.)

I will arrive at an answer when I try
to stand again. The sum may be the number of times I fail
to get up plus the number of pine needles
stuck like the dead in my flesh plus the smell of the coming
snow already buried in my skin.

BLUE

Give blueberries some sand, the memory of fire and they thrive
among oil jugs, air filters, mattress springs, a tire
divorced from its rim, its car,
the hard road, the rough rolling and throwing of gravel,
the speeding bitch behind the wheel — all of this makes picking
most difficult. The largest berries lie against the rubber wreath,
burst when touched, while others fall into the inner pool
where clouds of mosquitoes rise as a storm, the bites
strikes of lightning.

Back then I didn't think about it, but now I know
the tire didn't change itself just as the earth didn't
change position to accommodate a torn sidewall, nor plants
the hang of berry for this picking. How suddenly
things flatten. Year after year the perpetual
half-pail of berries, sunburnt welts, vicious dog-itch
are withstood with head down,
eyes ahead of hands and a mind
to pick only what's ripe among the junk.

EXPRESSIONS

It took an hour to pick enough blueberries,
write the word in juice, draw
the outline of your body on stone,
but there in the purple smear of burst skins
        the message echoes
the colour of the clouds that swarm the morning sun.
In the lake the sky floats
                face up and bruised.
We fight through the bush around the lake, view
the creation from the opposite shore, how small
our works become when divided. The whole
time the surface doesn't move,
holds the letters upside-down in the water.
Above the inversion of peace, the drawn body
stands at an angle, poised to fall.

THE ONE PSALM I KNOW

A song from the North

Still I am lost in the bush at sunset;
  2 Not moving.
  3 A hermit thrush splits the spring, its dusk, with a song
guides call ethereal,
  4 But it rises beyond heavenly notions
into nothing words can touch.
  5 On a dead branch its profile is a flat black blot
on a day fading, something the mind arranges into things
other than bird:
  6 A tent in summer, a warm back against the chest, the sweat
that slips between skins;
  7 A blueberry in fall, crushed between lips, its silent explosion
colouring the night, embedding shrapnel in my soul;
  8 A trail in winter, the hunt, the still heart of deer.
  9 This journey with psalm in pocket, a breeze
slight as unwanted breath on the neck, in the ear,
always ending in darkness, this familiar place.
  10 High notes part a lonely throat, portend
no safe way back to the road home.

ULTRASOUND

Under the moon moths and bats rip light
        into rags
            to clothe
this apparition.
        I lie on the ground and you return

as if nothing
        but the star's

position had changed.   Maybe
        some closet is still

full of your belongings, or
        you forgot

to take something along, like
        the silk
    you wore the night
        you went into labour,

        the tab
off a can from the first trip south,

        the butt
from your last cigarette,

    but nothing so sentimental
      remains —
just the boxed-up
    fear of things

      returning
as millions of moths
    drop
from flight
    like adjectives
      from a coward's pen
to escape
    ultrasonic waves
      teeth
        the inevitable
sight of your face.

FLOAT PLANE OVERHEAD AT 5 AM

In the space between sleepiness and sleep it's always
spring. The daily load of Americans is flying
over town, fish already in their eyes. Only
part of me wakes, but I hear what
the dream half hears: the slap of tails and gills
as fish fall flopping on the street. Torn
bits of fins hit the window and slide down.
Slime leads the sun to our eyes. Look up,
somehow their visions of fish have entered
our nakedness, lie with us on our sheetless bed.

Yesterday a man from Nevada asked me
where to fish, where to find the big ones,
what kind of bait gets the most bites. Still
I hear the accent, the boots striking the dock
as he walked away, his thanks echoing
off the rocks on the other shore.
This morning it's resounding. I wonder
how long it will continue, how long we'll lie
polished as hooks in tackle, catching the light
amid lead weights and rusty spoons.

A FEED OF FISH

Bait . . .

On the rocks fish heads gather,
act out the word *decay*,
wishing they had drawn *spawn* or *swim*
or decided not to play.
Some games go on forever.

I stand with net in hand, watch the suckers run.

. . . The Hook

Sucker belly chum, a trout's weakness,
an appetite driving through a slum,
the hook a risk buried in flesh
waiting for a tug. As hand
shadows ripple on the surface
the fish below come to know
why pimps in boats on northern lakes
don't wear pink.

. . . Catch

One pays the price for opening one's mouth:
reeled to the surface
            forced to suck new air
                        flop in the inability to breathe
            feel a finger forced in a gill
the rip of tissue in the bottom of the mouth
where the spike pokes through.
Life becomes time on a stringer,
floating belly-up beside an anchored boat.

There's nothing like a sharpened filleting knife,
the clean slice through
slime, scale and cool twitching flesh
that misses the smooth rope of guts
God forgot to braid. It takes time to learn
how to grip slippery things,
rip them out intact.

...And Release

The recipe for baked lake trout
calls for one whole fish.
              How will I fit
the lake into the pan? I close
the oven door and watch mud
ooze out. A thick black greens
the floor as if no longer wanting to
absorb years of loons and bugs and skeletons,
knows it already carries too much
weight on its bottom.

Garnish the dish with a lake's reflection
    and serve.

In my belly the fish acts out
a word nobody sees.

ALONG THE SHORELINE

The old jacket we fished out of the water
still hangs in the tree, red cotton fading in the sun.
To think something so waterlogged could ever dry out.
Ross Lake compels a traveler to leave material behind; often
things wash up between cattails, heavy and bloated.

It was here, so many years ago, we threw rocks
onto the rotting ice, trying to break through the last spring scab.
You lost a glove, said it was swallowed by snow and
left for university the next day, for good, each spring sending north
the skin of you to visit, stretched across somebody else.
     I wasn't fooled.
The one who showed me how to pull suckers out
by hand as they run upstream to spawn, the one
who built an ice shack out of a cardboard box when we were four,
should know how to skip a stone and how to wait
for the descending twang of ice to hit its own echo.

When you returned after finishing your first year, we searched
for a common body in silence, in the growing heat,
but it wasn't until midsummer that we saw the past bobbing
in the weeds offshore, learned words are gaffs that rip right through.

2'

FROST SHADOWS

Frost shadows gather on the windowsill, the generations
magnified, belying a convexity; certain patterns become
distortions as the window chatters and moves before the sun.
With a fingernail I plow through opacity, its thickness,
and leave behind a clear glass path. Through it I can see
enough to know what I am looking at.
It's been thirty years since I've seen
anyone stick a tongue to metal and scream
ah ah ah without words. The last victim I froze to
memory held my eyes as he stood, tongue glued
to the homeroom window, the teacher staring back
with chalk brush in hand, as if she was planning to
somehow erase the fear from inside. That kind of panic,
spreading like blood on ice, finds its way into every winter,
and in this room, within my chest, I feel again
the *tug tug tug* of stuck tongue.

Drawing on What's Left

The sun draws a rough sketch of willow, a map
on the snow with no directions. How to read it?
Chickadees hop between light and dark,
feathers matching drifts, the seed
scattered between the shadow lines.

It's still 40 below, cold as our bed. The sky is
clear and empty as conversation, your last words
buried under three feet of snow.
Things haven't changed since the door slammed shut.
Each day I sit alone, eye the birds, try
to look at the sunrise beyond the icicles
that hang like hope from eaves,
point at the broken ones below.

CAMOUFLAGED

Snow under willow, white feather mounds or faith:
                    this track's end could be
feathered feet under sleeping birds; a flock
so like the freshly fallen snow might
wait, eyes closed, a dozen hearts
beating in burrowed holes.

The ptarmigan came back again this winter — I put this in a letter
along with a photo of one peeking in the window at the cat
and a coupon for antifreeze clipped from a flyer sent from a store
down south, as if the six hour drive is worth the dollar.

You still invite me, though I think you know I'll never come.
Sometimes in the morning it's possible
to believe the city is closer,
the winding drive between tree and lake
a kind of retreat,
or the ptarmigan's burst into flight to be the sky
wanting its blizzard back.
But as the day goes on everything becomes
a long ways away,
an icy road no one wants to travel,
each move a potential wrong
step a bit too close to things that flee.

SNOW SQUALLS

Morning changes after you leave. Every morning,
an aging woman the sun must fear
peeks, one-eyed, at the backside of winter
through a half-closed blind. What burden
visibility heaps on shoulders in late winter squalls.

In the driveway snow curls around your footprints, as if it has fallen
asleep, as if each imprint of a foot walking away
were a pillow. Things look the same then.
The storm has lasted for days. It snows, too,
but we don't notice the drifts until you drive through them.

I'll always hear those tires driving over snow, the cadence.
Nights filled with words repeated still spill onto the day.
Head south then, I'd say, and over and over
I'd roll. *Good luck finding a job down there
that pays this kind of money*, and over I'd roll again.

Reciting Frost poems doesn't keep things from melting;
there's no more end rhymes in these hangover dreams.
Hope freezes again in moments after waking, after seeing
nothing but tire track wrinkles down the road.

Take Deep Breaths

Winters, pickpockets in white, take breath after breath unnoticed
from those too cold to know they've been robbed.
Still rock surrounds the house we built, like it always has, as if
waiting out criminals holding hostages inside.
Under the snow, beneath these feet, roots push cracks apart. There,
stashed ferns, moss, mid-winter images of them, of you, meet
the blessing of a hard edge, the matter of erosion.
These things I know.

It's during a climb in the cold, when pulse escapes
the bounds of body, when suddenly branches and needles
lub-dub above and shivering birds bury their heads
under wings to escape the noise, that something snaps,
not like the rifle shots of deadwood in the old burn on a February
night or the lake-ice bone-snap before break-up,
but louder — the sound of a neck twenty years later

as I look back at the house, its emptiness, at footprints pressing
snow like a pillow over the rock face until I go limp.
No longer can I move ahead, no longer can I breathe.

SQUIRRELED AWAY

ᘓᘔ

This yard, pocked with snow holes
from which squirrels pop out erect,
flashing earth-red fur, throbs
with the hurried rub of a body in a tunnel.

It moves into the shrinking
curve of my empty stomach,
the assimilation, the acid ache
when there's nothing left to absorb.

The tracks are ulcers left behind.

Nothing's like the feel of being peeled like hide
the morning after sleeping skin to skin,

yet, there's this:
my gut always tightens around the squirrel's chatter
when it shoots up from the hole it dug through winter.

I want to be that tunnel's light, to feel
the fur move through.

CRSO

Two hundred years to grow into a tree so deformed.
It takes just a moment to split it. A gust
        smacks the snowy crown on the rock
        like a hammer in a judge's hand.
This tree of carved heart, my first love's initials, is still
                connected where it snapped.
                It becomes a new corner
in a squirrel's winter road.
Over the gouges the animal runs
as it empties its downed cache
        stashes frozen mushrooms
        saws off iced cones with teeth
sharp as good-byes and hauls them along
                        with memories
up the trunk of another tree.

Blueberry scat studs the trail from the road to the cabin.
That was our last fall. It is winter now but
      everywhere I smell green things dying,
      everywhere the chatter of squirrel
reminds me of what's to come. There it is,
the animal that stashes things away.

All fall it hangs mushrooms in the trees, the heads
the colour of skin when the liver fails. There's one
for every organ wasted, the crooks of branches
              holding them
as the flesh quakes in the wind and dries out.

All fall it gnaws off cone-filled branches,
      lets them drop,
           stores them in the attic
as if they were bits of memory yet to be eaten.
The ceiling sags under all that weight.

Now the squirrel comes and goes like seconds
slowed to an excruciating pace.
Every time it emerges from the hole, it finds my eye.

Snow Angel

Snow angel, with every flake of snow you fade,
reflect more light. Familiar, the depth of sweep
now shallow, the wing's peripheral edge
softened by wind that swept away laughter
along with snow.
                  I'm thinking of all the times
we ripped across the ice, the open water,
turned our machines into the drift's curl without
rolling, built fires on the ice to warm our feet.
Before breakup we'd pull fish out of holes just to watch
eagles pick them off the ice. The birds threw
the bluest shadows when they flew away.
Or the time we were caught in a blizzard, when you
fell and swept the snow into an angel that
disappeared as soon as you stood up. You said
all you needed to know about winter you'd learn
lying on your back. Within the year you
married, turned from friend into
father. Before long the blowing snow settled
into this dull ache. We go fishing now and then,
snowmobile around a swamp full of it;
under its weight willows slump like piles of angels
slain to allay some dreaded disease.
Amidst all this I move, a side I barely see
still pressed in snow.

THE END OF THE ROAD

Know the full extent of the place
where ravens end up fighting
on the sidewalk over fish guts
massed like a brain,
a lake's ideas frozen in a pail.
Footprints to and from the neighbour's
broke through snow that's so hard bird's feet
leave no mark. The yard is packed
with vehicles of family and friends
in town for the long weekend.
The house barely stifles its laughter
as I go through the routine: unplug the truck,
throw my lunch on the seat,
start the stiff engine, scrape the windshield
while the truck warms up.
Through the exhaust I can see the birds,
I can smell the pickerel frying.

ECTOPIC BEATS

what is the time remaining if not January's——variant bird-

gaze beyond wingtips——the feathers's migration over time

as they became light——perfectly

arranged like daydreams before doubt grew new skin——or us

when waking up was joy——not this blank stare——this grief

fledged but moulting——fall plumage dull as grass in drought——

so apt to adapt to loss——this eulogy birds write with goaded squirrel

in a moment's——blurred scurry——across——a trail of branches——

as if the birds saw your mouth over a limp sparrow's bill——how little

puffs failed to make it breathe——your reflection dulls in the window

this loss——a dirty pane——the feather smudge where flight ended

PARTS OF A FEATHER

a) barb

> (the point, a process, the beginning of grief,
> its end stuck with blood to glass
> at 9:45 AM, when the bird hit, when I felt it
> leave this behind)

b) rachis

> (holds everything together like a mother, even here —
> a relationship with a window assumes an axis,
> geometry, a prerequisite required — no matter what,
> the connection is permanent. Any alterations can be
> washed off, but only physically, and only
> when the weather warms up)

c) web

> (a series of barbs, arguments on a shaft, never clears the air,
> but captures it and lifts conversation into trade winds, into
> migration, moving in a cyclical, predictable way)

d) down

> (the under-plumage of a life
> or one never lived — how to tell the two apart?)

e) quill

> (something so hollow can stick to flesh. It can
> take flight and change. There's always a window. Separation.
> In part, a quill is the remains of what is no longer here.
> As a whole, it's a feather
> cemented to pane and topped with snow.
> A loss with sun on it.)

At the End of February Things Weaken

Under certain weight, structures fail, roofs cave in
like so many metaphors, with a rafter's snap,
the buckle of beam, an avalanche of snow.
We didn't think it would happen to us.

Everyone said they saw it coming.
The roof rippled and sagged, shingles curled
like tongues repeating secrets hundreds of times,
the tar beaten out of them. No one said a thing.

We imagined the drifts on the roof
were mountain peaks, the swirls of blowing snow
apparitions of climbers lost, the moments
they tumbled down slope passing
like splinters of bone through skin.

Imagination is so unlike a camera, common sense.
Remember the documentary on Everest?
Men climbing what looked like a breast dipped in whipped cream
complained about wind, shortness of breath. I felt the same
when I looked on the roof and saw your back's arch
cast in snow. I should have known then
everything would come crashing down.

More Than Three Feet of Ice

How white this cheek of lake, though, broken
by knuckles of rock, pocked with yellow holes, ice shacks
spitting smoke
        trees like knives
pictured in the back of outhouse magazines.
It's not unblemished, melts a little under
fires that burn where skidoo tracks end.

It could be snow's reflection in glasses, vision
scarf-breathed — understanding, fog, a skinned skull
and a toque away, a wool rash, a frozen itch or

the right-left crunch of fear, the possibility
one could break through then sink beneath
the ice foundation — life, nothing more
than a leather mitt's slip, a brief frantic grasping,

but less obvious, perpendicular, an auger's twist,
ice-scrape echoes, the sudden gush
when curved blade cuts into water.

Nearly Drowned

Hundreds of wings thrash the light, brushing its truth
through bough-sprung snow. Spruce shelter the hip high bush;
in the sun needle tips drip. Last night it was not birds, but
a flock of us who fed upon each others
recollections, the pooling fruit, as if all
things could be consumed and mastered.
Water filled us. Yes, it's been said,
everyone drowns at some point. Beneath
the surface, the bug rippled reflections, currents
will grab at life and pull it under.

Winter, too, makes its claims. Through the ice
much is lost. Years ago I learned to chop holes,
gauge thickness, as if anyone can calculate
the weight a frozen body will bear. Still, I pause after
each step, my shadow stretching like a muscle as I look
for cracks, the weak patches, the open water snow hides.

I first fell through when I was nine, watched my breath
bounce against the ice, its rotten backside,
its sun-bubbled crust. That's all I can remember
about that March. Fear inhaled, like water, might forever
displace air from the lungs and, ultimately, the body
will cease to breathe. I think this as I snowshoe
through the woods, far from any open water.
                    It's only February, yet
as I stand in the bush among waxwings
lifting berries, as the sun pushes yellow-tipped tails
into my eyes, I find myself sinking.

BENEATH THE SKIN OF A DEER

This morning, a new beginning, warms as quickly as a hand
peeling back the hide of a fresh-killed deer, as if desire
wields a steel blade that separates
the pale veined layer from the meat.

A doe hanging from birch, head down, eyes wide
as a thief's caught running from the scene, may be
food for winter, bear bait for spring, slippers to silence
pursuit, more bones to polish under the coming August sun,

but the body foreshadows an end
with hair matted around arrow. It's like this:
to twist the shaft is to twist the heart, to pull it out
means nothing. Blood should sodden the snow,
but blood in the dead gels in vessels
far from the heart. Pump an artery slit,
see what darkness blobs out.

Free of the deer, the hide in snow finally stiffens.
In the dead's steam, raw smells rise as the naked animal
seeps then freezes, an existence skinned, knife-nicked.

TRACKING

This is your forest, your road. Diagonal striped by spruce-split sun, I move from darkness into light to find darkness again, breaking through breath-shadowed drifts. It was here you taught me how to measure the distance between each set of tracks, estimate the speed at which the animal traveled, reach beyond my child eyes into the sight of what had passed. In time, you said, I'd understand what steps displace. It's been thirty years, yet the space between the road and the walls of spruce, between the worm-browned branches weighed down by yesterday's flurries, remains beyond dreams of knowing.

Halfway down the road there's a curve: snow condom-studded, frost latexed over semen ribbons. Nearby footprints face a ditch, a yellow hole, a drip-line that thins before the toes. Between tire tracks another hole where exhaust ate the snow down to the sand.

Wolf tracks pass by all of it, heading north, the stride length shrinking just before and exploding just after this place, as if the smell of some desire frozen over had given chase. At the end of the road the trail penetrates the bush. There alder twigs hang broken.

Paper Dolls in Winter

A string of paper dolls stands in snow
(the trick is to wet them first, freeze flat, then erect)
hold hands through this morning's flurries,
remain expressionless as snow
buries them up to their chests.

This is what I did to pass the time between blizzards,
redirect memory's drifting snow, survive another
winter without you in this bride-white world
where innocence, like scissors, cuts perfect figures out of guilt.
Out in the cold, in the storm's accumulation, the relationship
remained frozen, linked through the winter by bits uncut.

Now the days are longer. I make snowballs, or boulders
(depending on the perspective), to pelt what I had cut out.

3'

SCARS

Tonight there's no nighthawk, no bedtime spine-scrape song.
Empty, the sky, my heart draining into it.
I don't know what to do with the silence,
                    with all its space.
The dark feels like a body's scars,
tight and smoother than creek stone.
Chicken pox, scalpel, filleting knife, the rock
on the shore of the Grass River, all
left marks that never went away.
                    Glorious under the touch
is the skin of the healed, but the gouge love digs in a body
never fills in. Like this, the place ripped open
when I first heard the bird sing. The wound weeps
as the rasp rubs down the flesh; now its absence grinds
the night into muscle, deepening this black spruce ulcer.

LESSONS OF TYRELL LAKE

Never wipe your ass with fire moss. It is not forgiving.
Fever rises from ash, from moss, an unstoppable blaze.
I heard it happened to a geologist just before
the fire swept through. At night he'd roll
around in his tent, trying to put himself out.
Rumours spread about a forest set in its ways, intolerant
of those who keep picking, and willing to torch
the ones who lack respect.

CRSO

Here, in the charred bark silence, memory stokes
unending fire underfoot. The breath of it
pushes up dust, clouds every chequered step.
Shadows fall hard in the morning's dead light and break
branches nested in the remains. Illogical black stumps oppose
what is green, shallow-rooted, barely moving. I haven't learned
how to run from flames, the forest's crowning — the captured know
the object of the flame and how this smoke king moves and why
a stalemate smells of dew-soaked soot. Try to remember this:
if you step on a square of light, a jump into ash will surely follow.
I look back, see nothing moving, nothing moved.

FIGHTING FIRE

Black spruce, black spruce, a fire mantra.
Everything has burned, the shield bared.
Now black sticks poke the sky like some gang
        after nothing.

Remember the way fire leapt over the night
as if memory had mixed up
Jack and the candlestick, the way you whispered
be nimble, be nimble, but not so quick, the way
the wind turned and pushed the fire away
from the hill we sat on and how your hair
blew forward like a blaze?
        The forest's heat was nothing.

After we left the wind turned again.

CASUALTIES

Wind twists black spruce like arms and they snap.
The ditch is a waiting room, the forest a body burned.
It's been a stormy summer. Hundreds of lightning strikes
set fire to more than trees.

Smoke mushrooms across the lake
where our cabin used to be, where we pulled bones
out of pickerel, watched a bear seek the guts
you said you didn't leave onshore.

Waterbombers trudge across the sky
with the weary hum of mourners.
Rain clouds on the charred horizon head
the other way, shadow the remains of what we built.
Firefighters stand in a blackened ditch,
watch us pass as if we were ash,
lean against the wind on spades.

Near Spring

Water piddles down the street, pavement dark as a drunk's crotch.
Everywhere sparrows hop toward their manic pecking.
You used to call the fox sparrow spring's rusty spasm,
its crazy kick of leaves akin to Morse code.
In depressions it leaves nothing to decipher. You taught me
to touch the space birds clear, to feel the bit of earth
they bare. You showed me how a pinch of it holds
together like a new day or hope; pressed too hard
the edges crumble. There, things begin to fall apart.
I learned no matter the wish, no matter the grasp, too soon
the sparrows will move further north, the trickle will stop
and any soil still moist will dry.
It's been a year now. You had dirt in hand the day
the plane took off, the day the little hand waved goodbye
from the window above the wing, a wave so frantic
it looked as if the hand had been severed, as if
the prop had caught it and was flipping it about.
That day you let the dirt drop and I watched it land.

SEDIMENT

To walk barefoot after winter over this spring melt trench
edged with sand, its silt belly soft as
want under toes, to look back at the prints,
how the arch has fallen, how wide the foot,
how deep it now sinks, to see how much
has disappeared with the snow, is to move with
you inside me again.

Last year's grass blanketed with dust lies as flat as memory
over something once loved, the face of it greyed
over the seasons, every blade a million slivers
in my hand. There's always the urge to rake it up,
clip it, see if you're still there, but I fear
something else might be lurking underneath. It's the space

between things I fear, the four-dimensional expanse
between sky, grass and ground, sand and skin, breath and
breath, the apnea that brings on pathological
thoughts of a future alone, temporarily suspended, that become
this sinking underfoot, this silk shift.

CONSIDERING THE GARDEN TO BE WATERED

Don't envy this garden. Its swamp soil,
ever dry, always wants more water, as if a thirst
for what it was reaches deep like fever.
It's something to cover lightly, immerse in tepid bath,
handle with held breath and gloved hands.

Stand here if you will. Beyond hoed rows, you can see
the sun smack the backside of the horizon, hear a cry rise
and fall from where it came in silence. Sometimes it hurts
to look into the light, watch ants crawl into it and then over
the buds of this old peony; it was split from a division
sent from England after the war, a perennial
meant to brighten the north, celebrate
a new life as a miner, its pink blooms pale as a face
when the dust clears in a reoccurring dream.
Every year it grows back. Every year
the blooms droop as soon as they open.

Look at what I've grown. Stunted vegetables surround me.
From now on I'll let them self-seed. In ground left alone
things will grow, mature early. These days dreams, even imaginaion,
seem sprinkled from packets. What grows between frosts
manages only to bud. People grow what they can.

Every day there's a leaf by leaf examination and I never fail
to wish the placental slime on lettuce leaves were lit silk,
but it's nothing more than a trail of slug on its way to a dish of beer.
Every morning I dump slugs out. Before the temperature rises,
I connect the hose, bleed the air, watch spits blast the ground
until water flows back into the swamp.

That Which Seems to Grow Up Here

The prairie plants I remember were patient,
tolerant of an exploring child, willing
to baby-sit while gophers napped and red-tailed hawks
communed with clouds in rippled air.
Here nothing rests flat as a grass whistle between my thumbs,
or accepts the same space blown. It took twenty years of dreams

to learn how the north's thin acid soil hoards flora like a hermit,
how faint tracks of children deepen as they grow into unwilling
bodies then into ghosts who'll forever bounce from trunk to trunk
into clearings. Nowhere is the face of who I once was,
only a glimpse of hands holding a crocus posy, and below, a shadow
moving over the prairie, over the sun-ringed blackness of gopher holes.

CABIN FEVER SYMPTOMATOLOGY: A REOCCURRING PRAIRIE DREAM

Watch the creek spread the legs of the prairie.
Sweat beads on spear grass; the prairie pants
as the wind strokes her tight muscles, whispers
a direction in her ear.

The creek slips in the crevice
surrounded by skin pocked
with cow parsnip, angelica,
poison hemlock to find
she is fully dilated.

The creek nods with the sky
blue blooms of speedwell
as they reflect on the coming
waters, the finger ripples that guide
as she begins to push.

MISSING

Day 1
The wind is stronger this morning, flexing muscles.
Ravens admire the hard blue bulge
then disappear into the frayed edge of this forest.
No fairy tales here.
Someone is lost. A hollered name echoes off rock.

Day 3
Searchers walk, as evenly spaced as the bush will allow,
while dogs bay up ahead. Heads down, slow steps, voices
calling the same name over and over until it sounds
like something else. Nothing but trees ahead and pieces of blue
plate sky thrown against them.

Day 5
Another day, another bologna sandwich.
Bread spotted with mould. Meat pale and thin.
The name, said less, sometimes slips the mind.

Day 7
Not a footprint to be found. Bear sign all around, none to be seen.

Day 9
The forest thickens.

Day 11
It rains. The forest, yellow rain suits. Rubber boots on sponge
the only sound.

WATCHING TRAFFIC GO BY

Above Highway 10 a full moon cycles, pulling the sky behind
as if it were a baby in a wagon.
       Tonight is like the others.
Vehicles come and go,
windows fogged with hot chocolate steam.
Yet the rock glow pulls the darkness to the surface,
blackens the road between the double lines.
This is what light does.
       Under the moon I become old highway,
shoulders pounded out by heavy trucks,
surface broken by potholes and construction.
Here traffic should flow slow in the night,
but speed is all I know. Tail-lights disappear
around the curve the same way fury bends around
the semblance of calm. Each time the red dots vanish
I wonder if you've settled down,
       if you're ready for me to come home.
       I never know.
All I've learned after years of lying under the moon is that
fullness doesn't last and balance is senseless
unless you know how to ride along,
which way to lean.

RISE

1.

In a dream dough rises in a bowl. Over it Wittgenstein watches, says the only goal is understanding. *Get lost Ludwig. I said I don't need philosophy to make bread. Before you go, monitor the sense of this* (he looks at my middle finger, raises his eyebrows). I know it's all nonsense. A winter spent up here reaches deep into meaning, into explanations of it. Now desire is sun-leavened. The recipe (get up, moon the horizon, swell, ascend; never forget to knead; dream between risings) is not easy to follow. See how things turn out: March snow is doughy, wrinkled. The land, a belly sagging after shedding its weight, needs spring to nip and tuck and suck out winter's fat. What to do with all the skin?

2.

Wittgenstein shoos mosquitoes away, says this dream is nothing but a buzzing cloud of conceptual confusions. Maybe so. Do you want clarification? The fat of the land I am. Live off me. Whole-wheat, rye, pumpernickel — tell me what you want. A low fat greenstone sub? An ever sandwich with a little Dijon?

3.

Understanding is an ability you'll never possess, Wittgenstein says, poking at dough bubbles. I tell him I want to be a packet of yeast, a foil-lined keeper of unicellular ascomycetous fungi, to see not the broken bottles on the rocks. Isn't the future all about someone opening you, setting the conditions for you to learn how to convert sugar into alcohol and carbon dioxide? He shakes his head and throws the *Tractatus* at me.

4.

I want this place to be a slice of bread with jam on it. I want to be the knife spreading wild strawberry. *Think about the rules for the use of these words*, he says. *It's not about want.*

5.

As the bread bakes, Wittgenstein sits me down for the final exam. One multiple choice question worth 100% of the final mark:
Burnt toast and the Canadian Shield. Both
a) set off smoke alarms
b) shatter
c) made mouths water before things went wrong

I circle an answer.

The Hobbit in the Canadian Shield

You thought the book would be perfect to help me settle
in a place so hollowed out, so empty of you. Yet no wizard
colours the greenstone beneath these weary feet.
Just rock is all it is, something that cooled billions of years
before I walked here, and became hard as the heart in this chest,
a thing now beating on its own, a mass no one blasts through.

This may be fantasy, but after years of reading it over and over
I believe Tolkien penned more in hope
I fear is false as any bottom. In this chapter
I'm alone, here, because of you my motions
are automatic, emotions invisible. The ring I twirl
powerless.

DOWN THE SAME ROAD

The ditch has been full of water all along.
Across spruce reflections, rose petals float.
I know there's beauty in this, but I don't want to continue
to drive down this road, travel the graveled scratch
between mines in this forest, add another stone
to the cairn. The monument survived the year
like monuments do. Let's leave it alone. Its stability
will be compromised if we pile the rock too high.
But I know you'll add another, then remind me of where
you had stepped out the skid marks, measured paint
scrapes on the rock, gathered pieces of the headlight's
glass the morning after, and I'll watch birds look down
at their forms moving over the water, at the birds
who look back up, peeking around petals at their flight.

In Full Bloom

Conspiracy smells like flowers. Every bloom
holds between its petals a growing possibility.
From this garden I pull handfuls of chickweed as if it were hair.

Six weeks you've been fighting fire, the bush your wife.
A whiff of smoke is all I know anymore. It passes in wind
from the west, a wicked witch on a burning broom.

At night I imagine the sleeping bag you're in, the smell of it,
and in the dark I see too much inside. The poke of head
against the tent wall. Nylon on nylon's rhythmic rub.
The rip of zipper.

In the morning more flowers, more weeds, more pulling.

LARGE YELLOW LADY'S SLIPPER

In June we come upon the flower, its bright yellow bulge.
How it blends into shadow like sugar
in a drink, could soothe the parched
with one swallow, yet you like to guzzle
rare things through the eye until they're empty
while I watch.

Without a word its pouty lower lip begs you to come
closer, its brown spotted tongue the sign of a virus
I know you want to catch.
I imagine it licks every drop that oozes
from the swollen clouds, the thunderheads
purple and engorged to the point of bursting.

You know better than to touch, but still your hand
reaches out to stroke the bloom.

A CONTRACTOR

In the rocks a flock of pipits sings,
the clink of a million icicles.
It's summer's end. Migration. The job is done,
your bags are packed. I know another
life waits down south. Another
pair of arms will spread like wings
when you walk off the plane so dirty, but not
as dirty as you were

the other day when I watched you in the bank,
saw the way you signed the slip. The cursive
motion raised goose bumps. I wanted
to be that piece of paper you slid in
your wallet, next to the pictures I know must be there.
     The son,
       the daughter,
         the wife with hair like mine.

Two weeks at home then you fly north again.

ANOTHER GENESIS

Sun pounds on the morning with a swollen bloody fist.
I dig a grave, bury the cat named Eve.
Too many times the spade strikes rock, in the steel
I hear the dead cat's purr. Vibrations claw
the spine. I know you'll
miss her.

In three days you'll be home. Already
I imagine hard arms, log legs, a body moving over me,
but I don't know if it's yours.
Even memories of the cat kneading your belly
stop at the paws, as if the repeated poke
was all that mattered.

I can't see your face or recall the weight
your body pressed onto mine, or if it hurt
when the stick dug into my back that time
at the creek, but I remember the impressions
in my skin, the tracks the stick left
all the way up to my neck.
Your tongue touched every one. I still feel it
wiggling up against the abrasions.

AFTER A RAIN

In places a puddle dulls a depression, flattens
an elevation change with a sudden downpour.
A three-day rain corrals clouds on the pavement
in little groups like sheepdogs steered with silent whistles.

It's been raining forever. I straddle a puddle
to caulk a crack in the cinderblock foundation
where black ants pass like life and disappear.
I wish more would follow. Their burden
might be mine, each carrying off a bit
of the memory of buying this house when
the town was booming, even though
you said this crack would lead to ruin.
Every spring I watch you measure its length, its spread;
all year you must wonder its depth.

The neighbour's lab stops to lap the water at my feet,
pees on a poplar when he leaves and it's then it begins
to ooze out, the white goo, the feeling I've done this all before.
A wad of it plops in the puddle, just where I knew it would land.

WEEDING

A pile of dandelions wilts on the limestone path we laid
last summer and we lay down, too, after the last slab was dug
into the ground with dirt on our bellies and the little secret
stone that ripped you, the one I sucked clean and kept prisoner
between a willow twig and lady beetle wing. That stone grew
into so many rocks to walk on in this garden, stones blond
as hair, rough as hands pulling it.

The stones came from the crevices we leapt across.
It's been years, but I still see your foot slip off the mossy edge,
the grasp at whatever was close by, and it was fear
of a fall to a bottom we could not see that made us
hang onto a ledge we didn't know was there.

These days the path is overgrown, no stranger to the pulling.
Dirt holds rocks in place while we yank out yellow flowers,
watch roots break and ooze what's familiar on our hands.

PICTOGRAPHS IN THE MIDDLE OF LAKE X

In a dream *The Odyssey* wedged between rocks,
its cover soaked and swollen. Another translation
left in the rain by someone who must know better.
I look up and the lakeshore is library.
I'm wearing Homer's shoes.

Every day a new dream, a new language. I am words
on tongues of the dead, an endless poem
wanting to move, waiting for breath
until there's nothing left but bone.

I'm in the boat again, bobbing against an island.
Waves crash over the side, wet my shoes.
I promise not to tell anyone
about the pictographs, not even the one whose hands
will wake me.

Life After Mining

Needles and moss crushed together, held
in declining light, draw a bit of blood,
deepen underfoot the memory of green.

You're unsure of the light and where you'll go
when the place shuts down, is done with you—-
someplace where roaring is more lion,
less monster,
the glint, teeth instead of steel,
heart, a muscle in a body without ore,
where evening doesn't throw the mine's
shadows back as if it, like you, lost again
its sharp-nailed grip on the structures
you helped build, on the complex now
scabbing the surface of South Main.

Visions of a return to prairie escape
from dreams so rough with the north's rock
your eyes cannot close.
(You pull lids down and over
the forest and trees poke through skin.
No hurried morning storm,
no unbroken midday plate of sky,
no tears to wash away debris.)

Will you be remembered for as long as it takes
dynamite to drop a wall of rock?
A few moments of balance might remain
deeply pressed into the rotting forest floor.

Too Late to Make a Break For It

Something is moving under your eyelids, something removed.
You didn't want this life to end so far from where you were born
or so far from what you wanted to remember.
Fifty years have passed, yet this place is unfamiliar. Back then
you cut down trees to build the things you wanted to own.
A cabin, a dock, a bridge. You felled trees to burn
in the wood stove. Sometimes the wood was green and smoke
snaked through the forest as if it was trying to outrun
something much bigger. Over the water it disappeared.
On the surface, reflections of trees and sky, and below?
                        A northern lake can be that deep.
Like the rock under it, you cupped water, let it flow over you,
but none of it sank in. Fifty years and you never learned to swim.
It's too late now. You'll try to get away, but you'll leave too many
fingerprints behind, signs of things bungled. Now
        belongings are stolen without you knowing,
the thief's hands gloved in your skin.

Words to Another Forest Song

Sometimes a word can be heard over music,
needles twanging twigs
           branches drumming air
                beating on neighbouring trees,
but rarely does its meaning find volume.

Long, this hum — a hum strung like a wood thief's rig
down the throat's slope and wired in the belly
where hewn words slide along fearful of getting caught
in the old growth, in memory so tangled, in the moss-
soft notes rising from the understory.

It is song for the senses. A forest deep reflects
in the eyes of squirrels and, beyond, a clearing slices
pupils into pieces of hard candy light, a humbug
too sharp to suck, too sweet to leave behind.
Even when I fill my mouth with pine needles the taste remains
and desire finds a way in — like an ant on a scent trail
        it follows no bounds, knows nothing of closed lips.

Here is the whole composition, its elements
wild notes struck; each tone — the rake of bark under bear claw,
the plop of water closing in on a frog's escape, the sinking
of marsh marigold pollen — vibrates in the space left
between petals and the surface of what I don't know.

Sources

The following books helped me imagine the transient voices in these poems — voices that call out or fall to silence in Canada's provincial norths:

"Northern Visions: New Perspectives on the North in Canadian History. eds. Kerry Abel and Ken S. Coates. (Peterborough: Broadview Press, 2001). The epigraph on page 8 is taken from the introduction to this book and reprinted by permission of Broadview Press.

The Forgotten North: A History of Canada's Provincial Norths. Ken Coates and William Morrison. (Toronto: James Lorimer & Company, Publishers, 1992).

The Historiography of the Provincial Norths. eds. Ken Coates and William Morrison. (Lakehead University: Centre for Northern Studies, 1996).

The epigraph to "Go Beyond" is from John V. Hicks' "Fantaisie" in *Overheard by Conifers* (Thistledown Press, 1996)

Acknowledgements

Some of these poems were first published in *Grain, The Harpweaver, In Medias Res, Kaleidoscope Journal, Other Voices, A Room of One's Own, Running Barefoot: Women Write the Land* (Rowan Books, 2001), *Urban Coyote: New Territory* (Lost Moose Publishing, 2003), and broadcast on CBC Saskatchewan "Gallery", and performed by Globe Theatre "On the Line". Thanks to the editors and producers.

"Ectopic Beats" was published by Greenboathouse Books as a limited edition broadsheet in 2003. Thanks to Jason Dewinetz and Aaron Peck.

An earlier version of this manuscript won the 2003 Alfred G. Bailey Prize and was runner-up for the 2004 John V. Hicks Manuscript Award. "Expressions" won the 2002-2003 Harpweaver Prize, the Canadian Authors' Association Prize for Poetry.

Thanks to the Saskatchewan Arts Board for providing assistance in the writing of this book, the Saskatchewan Writers Guild for its programming, and the Saskatchewan Writers/Artists Colony for the space and time to write.

I'm grateful to those who have read these poems and supported their development. Special thanks to my mentor Gerald Hill and to the writers and artists at St. Peter's Abbey. Many thanks to everyone at Thistledown Press and to my editor, John Lent.

Thanks to Judy de Mos and Ariel Gordon for the daily exchange. Thanks to my family. Most of all, thank you Harvey Schmidt.